BE
BRILLIANT
IN THE
BASICS

BE
BRILLIANT
IN THE
BASICS

FINDING SUCCESS IN RETAIL THROUGH DETAIL

KELVIN GOSS

BROWN BOOKS
PUBLISHING GROUP

Be Brilliant in the Basics
Finding Success in Retail Through Detail

Brown Books Publishing Group
16250 Knoll Trail Drive, Suite 205
Dallas, Texas 75248
www.BrownBooks.com
(972) 381-0009

A New Era in Publishing®

ISBN 978-1-61254-939-2
LCCN 2016953355

Printed in the United States
10 9 8 7 6 5 4 3 2 1

For more information or to contact the author, please go to www.BeBrilliantInTheBasics.com.

This book is dedicated to all retail leaders who refuse to settle for poor to average performance!

Special thanks to the moms who teach and instill in us the Golden Rule at an early age and that there is no expiration date to it!

Love you, Helen Goss, Maxine Madkins, Norsha Lynn Delk, and Yvonne Antoinette Woodhouse Delk.

TABLE OF CONTENTS

FOREWORD

Kelvin Goss has over thirty years of retail experience. He began his retail career as a teenager, bagging groceries and selling hot dogs at a hot-dog cart. He was the first African American promoted to vice president of a regional grocery chain, and he then advanced his career by moving to Walmart, the largest retailer in the world.

His passion, energy, and understanding about what it takes to succeed in retail literally jump off the pages of this book. Retail is detail. Retail is all about interpersonal relationships—with associates, customers, peers, and supervisors. Kelvin delves into the intricacies of being a servant-leader with practical tips about how to succeed as a retail-store manager.

Kelvin takes readers on a journey from the initial interview process to the first day on the job to the rewarding promotion to store manager. Each chapter provides insights on how to excel and stand out. Making a good first impression, knowing when to blend in and when to stand out, and how to invest in yourself are just a few of the golden nuggets inside this treasure trove of thoughtful, practical advice.

The goal of this book is to place you, the driver, on the fast-paced retail HOV (high-occupancy vehicle) lane so that you can achieve your career aspirations and succeed beyond your wildest dreams.

Buckle up, and enjoy the ride!

SHARON ORLOPP

Retired Global Chief Diversity Officer, Walmart

PREFACE

From an early age, I had a passion for retail. While shopping in the local hometown grocery store with my mom, I would drift away from her and walk every single aisle, admiring all the products and packages. When I was twelve, we lived in Wolfe City, a town with a population of sixteen hundred in the northeast corner of Texas. After school, I would stop by the local grocery store, which was no more than twenty-thousand square feet, and gaze at the canned goods. I'd carefully turn each can so the labels were facing the right way. The manager, Bill Daniels, never ran me off. He would just chuckle at how long it took me to straighten up a four-foot section of items. I felt a sense of belonging in that I was helping all the customers who came to shop the store by ensuring all the labels were facing the same direction.

My passion and my understanding of how important retail was to the public and the employees who worked hard to make the store look good grew daily. I would ask the manager to hire me nearly every day; and by virtue of my persistence, he finally did when I turned sixteen (I imagine I was also getting on his last nerve). I developed a love for the retail business and wanted to truly become a student of retail. I started as a sacker who bagged groceries and took them to the customers' cars. I had various roles in the store: selling hot dogs, stocking shelves, cashiering, and ordering products. So began my thirty-six-year career in retail, from sacking groceries in a mom-and-pop grocery store to overseeing stores across a third of the United States—approximately 1.8 million square miles—for the world's largest retailer.

In every position, at every retailer, my goal was to be an outstanding employee who made a difference in the results of the store and the experience of the customer. I made many mistakes as a leader, but I reflected and learned from each one. Early on, I realized as a retail leader that I didn't have to have all the answers, but I had to truly understand the basics of leadership, become brilliant in them, and enjoy the career path I had chosen. I learned to be humble, accept feedback, seek insight, and invest in my personal development. I also saw the power of networking knock down Goliath-like obstacles. By applying these lessons, my personal career soared to new heights.

I had often wished there was a GPS system for retail leadership, something to give you some clear turn-by-turn guidance from day to day, so that you could avoid accidents or obstacles, know when to exit an idea, and understand how to merge back on the road without any negative impact to your career, the organization, or those you lead.

In March 2015, while returning from my mother's funeral in Texas, I reflected on the need for such guidance. You see, my mom had taught school for well over thirty-five years in Texas, and she'd left a legacy with so many people (myself included) through her qualities as a teacher. Looking out the window on the wing of a jet at thirty-five thousand feet, I knew I wanted to pass on knowledge just like my mom had done—something that could have a positive impact on many people. As I gazed out that small plane window, I realized I'd had many teachers in my life. I'd seen brilliant retail leaders over the years teach employees, just like students, how to be successful and make retail a career. As I reminisced in midair on those instructive relationships, I had an epiphany: I could capture all I had learned in one book and pass on the insight to people who have chosen to take the unique ride of retail leadership. It dawned on me in that moment that I had gone from having a staff meeting with ten employees in Wolfe City, Texas, to having staff meetings, presentations, personal conversations, and lunches with senior leadership and CEOs of Fortune 500 companies. I would not let all of these conversations expire upon my retirement like so many retail leaders have done.

Before the wheels hit the tarmac from that flight, I had jotted on a napkin, "So you think you want to work in retail leadership? Then be brilliant in the basics." The book in your hand was born!

As I walked through the terminal, I thought about one of the most inspirational leaders I have ever had the privilege to work with as a peer. I knew she had a tremendous amount of experience in retail from various organizations and could contribute insight that would be so valuable to those who would be looking to have a successful career in retail leadership. I also knew she was currently a leader at one of the most respected retail grocery companies in the United States. This would also allow the insight of brilliant leadership behaviors to be shared from both male and female perspectives. I reached out to her, and she was thrilled at the idea of coauthoring a book that could positively impact people on a career path in retail. Felicia Delk's journey started similarly to mine, as a teenager with a desire to make some extra money and deliver great service that left people with a smile and coming back for more.

KELVIN GOSS

If you were to research the name Felicia, it means happy, which is a sentiment that aligns with my desire to ensure world-class customer service is delivered. At the age of sixteen, when I started my first retail job inside of Chesapeake Square Mall in Chesapeake, Virginia, I had the opportunity to meet and interact with a diverse group of people and began to learn how a business operates. The lessons I learned as a teenager in high school working at A&W Hot Dogs as a shift manager opened my eyes to the possibilities of running my own shop or retail store.

While in college, I had a desire to learn a different facet of retail and started as a part-time associate at Kirkland's in Greenbrier Mall. My journey from part-time associate to store manager was fulfilled with a richness of knowledge from several mentors. I view retail as an opportunity to connect with people and deliver on a service while building personal wealth. In my retail career, I have had the opportunity to work for some well-known companies with strong brands. I currently have the privilege to oversee Talent and Development for over one hundred stores in the world's largest grocery retailer. As I advanced up the ladder (I am still climbing), I was faced with barriers that sometimes required the assistance of others to break down. This book is designed to assist you with identifying those obstacles and finding solutions to problems by being brilliant in the basics.

FELICIA DELK

We are confident that once you read this book, you will be inspired to apply many of the suggestions and best practices that can help you "Be Brilliant in the Basics of Retail Leadership." We have had the privilege to enjoy careers with top organizations that are prominently listed on Fortune's Top 500 companies list. No matter the profession, we all have the ability to teach others with our life experiences. We truly wish you the best in your retail leadership career.

By reading and applying the insight shared in this book, you can expect to understand the importance and principles of being stage ready, of being agile, of being knowledgeable about your business, and of how communication and networking adds value to your leadership.

In the appendix, we share exercises for each chapter that will help you practice and internalize the leadership principles presented in this book.

Brilliant leaders are proactive and know the importance of accountability for self and those they lead. Most importantly, to be brilliant in retail basics you must possess in your leadership the characteristics of servant-leadership! Now let's zoom in on being stage ready!

1

BE BRILLIANT IN STAGE READINESS

If you have taken an interest in the title of this book, that is outstanding; you are to be commended because that means you have a desire to be Brilliant in the Basics of Retail Leadership.

Life is about choices; we make many every day. Some people on their jobs or in their careers choose to be poor performers for whatever reason, some choose to be average, and some choose to be above average. However, in my experience of thirty-five plus years in retail, there are an elite few who choose to find the answers to "How to Be Brilliant in Retail Leadership." When done right, it is like poetry in motion to observe their characteristics, behaviors, conduct, and speech on a daily basis as they interact with employees and consumers. It becomes almost second nature to them to put W's in the Win column on every project or goal they set for themselves or the retail organization. The reason? It's simple: They choose to be Brilliant in the Basics of Retail Leadership.

If you have a desire to be highly successful in retail as a retail leader, then this Brilliant in the Basics book is for you! If you want to improve your personal brand as a retail leader, then this Brilliant in the Basics book is for you! If you want to improve your chances for career growth and financial reward and positively impact your company and its bottom line, then this Brilliant in the Basics book is for you!

We plan to inspire you to choose to be Brilliant in the Basics of Retail Leadership. This choice can assist you in having a successful, strategic career in an industry that many choose for employment. Unfortunately, some fall short of Brilliant Leadership, which impacts them personally, their employees, and, ultimately, the company and its shareholders if applicable.

Retail leadership can be compared to a breathtaking roller-coaster ride.

Imagine being on one of the world's greatest roller coasters, and you have the very front seat. The moment you got in that seat, all eyes were on you, and there is a nervousness because of what is ahead, up the hill, around the corner, and often in the dark; however, you chose to get in that seat knowing you could expect to go slow or speed up, with possible sudden and unforeseen drops, dramatic curves, steep obstacles to climb, precipitation, or high headwinds that take your breath away. But you have mentally prepared yourself for this ride. Come what may, you are going for it, eyes wide open (most the time), even if you have to scream from anxiety or anticipation of what is about to happen. Your emotions could possibly range from extreme nausea, fear, and sadness to happiness and being overjoyed with tears of great satisfaction from what you have just experienced.

The metaphor you just read, in my experience of thirty-five plus years in retail, is the best possible way to describe retail leadership. When you take on the role of becoming a leader in retail, it is an amazing experience, even considered breathtaking at moments. Like the roller-coaster ride just described, you will experience many emotions the moment you get in the retail leader front seat, where all eyes are on you! You will on any given day feel as though you have just hit a dramatic curve, endured a sudden drop, with high headwinds coming at you through multiple assignments at once, when whatever could go wrong went wrong at the worst possible time of an important visit from your boss and their boss (even the best umbrella can't stop you from getting drenched). However, you also can experience the most beautiful view from the very top when you are Brilliant in the Basics of Retail Leadership. Because of your execution and being brilliant in certain leadership characteristics, you will have a chance to be on the very top and experience a view like no other.

To get to the top takes work and endurance, but the ride is well worth it. When you are on top, you look forward to your evaluation, you look forward to the incentive attached to your base salary, and you look forward to visits from your boss and their boss because you are stage ready and have something to show! When you are on top, you scream with excitement and the environment in which you work is super exciting and fun, filled with like-minded employees who enjoy being on top with you. You have infused those around you to know what is expected to get to the top; getting there in the front seat makes a difference in what you see and how you are seen! They know that you appreciate and understand that you are on top because of the way you inspire and treat them. They want you to enjoy and be on top often if not always! You are on top because you have communicated effectively, set reasonable expectations, and held your team and yourself accountable to deliver on goals and exceed customers' expectations. You are on top because you were brilliant at networking to get to the front seat and people believed you were the right choice to be in it. The awe-inspiring retail leadership roller coaster is a great ride to be on, but the experience is totally different when you are on top!

One thing for sure about the retail leadership roller coaster and the actual roller coaster that is absolutely 100 percent factual is that there will always be someone else who wants to take your top spot by coming from behind. Don't allow this to cause you to fret, dear friend; when you put into practice the basic simple truths and best practices in this book, you truly will have the capabilities to visit that top spot more often. In addition, you will enjoy the retail leadership ride and the view that will give you personally, your team, your customers, and your company the most rewarding experience!

STAGE READINESS

Continuing with the metaphor of roller coasters discussed earlier, where are they typically found? You got it: at amusement parks. If you were to visit Southern California or Orlando, Florida, you would have no problem getting directions to the Happiest Place on Earth, Disney. You can count on the fact that every single day they are open, their employees and the park are stage ready. You will never find a theme park character unprepared to deliver a legendary experience or the famous mouse on break with his head in his hands while he takes a reprieve. As a retail leader, you have to have the same mentality about yourself, your employees, and your store(s). Being stage ready will require some basic leadership qualities from you.

First, inspect what you expect. Every day you arrive at your location, plan to spend eight to twelve hours. Don't allow yourself to develop tunnel vision and solely see what you want to see (completely oblivious to clutter, dirt, dust, and sloppily dressed, unhappy employees that you are tasked to lead with no smile and no name badges identifying them as connected with your business). You have to view your store, your associates or employees, your office, your restrooms, your backroom, your break-room, and even your parking lot and sidewalks as being onstage every day you are open. A brilliant leader doesn't have to have his or her supervisor write them a list on a notepad or iPad that says, "Dust this, power wash that, sweep behind that, organize this, etc." Get the point? When put in charge, take charge. Set a precedent of what is acceptable and what is not under your leadership.

Second, you have to be cognizant that on any given day your supervisor, their supervisor, or even the CEO could come strolling in your location (announced or un-announced). It has been said that it takes ten good visits to make up for one bad visit that went horribly wrong. These are truly the days while you are in the middle of a supervisor's visit and you think, "Calgon, take me away." Whether there is truth to that or not, know this for sure: you, your store, and your employees are always onstage, under the spotlight, so to speak. A brilliant retail leader will have specific plans in place to be stage ready every day the business is open!

Third, a brilliant retail leader should put a cadence in place that ensures the basics of retail leadership take place day after day, no matter which leader opens or closes the business. This sequence would include a possible checklist until it is established as a culture and/or price of admission to be a leader. Certain aspects of the retail business that should be an expectation daily of a brilliant, stage-ready leader are as follows:

- The parking lot is clean and free of debris from open to close, and someone is responsible to make sure that is never an issue (including behind the store or location).
- The building should be clean, interesting, ever exciting, and merchandised from the front to the back to wow the customer with the right price.
- Listen to your customer feedback through the company's feedback process or by

polling them yourself. They will tell you honestly how you and the business are doing onstage and in the spotlight. Take action on what you hear!

- Restrooms, breakrooms, and offices must be immaculate—this sends a message to all employees that our standards are immaculate and nobody wants to be the one on the team to lower the standard.

- Every employee should have daily goals that they are enabled and obligated to deliver. They also should be able to clearly articulate what those goals are if asked and explain how they achieve them.

- Employees should have a natural smile and practice the age-old loft rule of speaking within the designated distance to a customer with a genuine hello and "How may I assist you?" Speak to your customers. It's the reason you have employment. Employees who missed this in onboarding or hesitate to practice this behavior, I can assure you, will be the ones scheduled during those horrible visits discussed earlier, and you won't be deemed brilliant as the one who hired or tolerates their behavior.

• Every single employee has to know what it is you stand for as the retail leader and what you don't. If you leave it to chance, you will never achieve consistent stage-ready culture.

Take this quick test. Call your leadership team into your office and ask this one question: What top three things do you stand for as leader in charge of the store? After they have written down their individual answers to your question, have them say out loud their answers. It will provide clarity on how aligned you are as a team on what is important. When all leaders are on the same page about what is most important, there will be a great chance it shows in your stage readiness!

These are basic best practices that are not carried out in the many retail stores today consistently, and the visit becomes poor to average for customers and supervisors. Once that average culture is firmly established, due to lack of brilliant leadership, it is incredibly difficult to change. It could take months to years to correct.

I know of a retail leader in Houston, Texas, who in 2003 had his district manager stop by his store almost every evening on his way home from visiting the other stores he oversaw. One day, after consecutive visits from the district manager in a week, the retail leader walked his district manager out to his car about 6:00 p.m. on a Thursday. He asked his district manager why he so frequently saw him in a week so late in the evening. The district manager smiled and said two things profoundly:

1. Brilliant leaders work when the business is heaviest to make sure the store is stage ready.

2. I stop by your store because I want to go home on a natural high—this store is exciting and the merchandise is displayed well, with the happiest employees I have ever seen interacting with customers.

I simply said, "Thanks, Mike! I appreciate the compliment and will pass it on to the team!"

The Disney example is great to follow in principle. Disney employees get it right every day, but that comes from clear direction, alignment, and commitment to be world class or brilliant! I'm sure the senior leadership at Disney takes days off from time to time, but you can't tell they are off by their stage presentation in the theme park. Their performance is the same level day in and day out! Brilliant leaders don't spend the majority of their time in the office looking at a computer. They are out on their stage touring, teaching, and setting expectations. They build a stage-ready culture one associate at a time. The investment of time to build a strong team through clear direction, alignment, and commitment will have a great return!

A leader that never gets surprised by the stage they are on will have a business rhythm that allows for an inspection in every area of their business from outside in the parking lot to the trash dump in the back of the building. A brilliant retail leader tours their location to teach so that the culture and expectations are sustainable.

All employees know their responsibility; they perform in their roles well because the brilliant leader hired the best employees they could find and set clear expectations. It takes discipline and diligence to get out of the office as a leader and to walk or tour the store/location—your stage—with a keen customer/retail leader eye. When leaders set a high expectation or standard in every area of the store/location you are privileged to lead and truly have a routine of inspecting what you expect from your employees, you reduce the risk of your stage not being ready. Ultimately, your supervisor, their supervisor, or the CEO shouldn't be your biggest concern. It truly is your customers who vote with their dollars (wow them daily like Disney); you will see brilliance in the culture you inspirationally developed through a team of engaged employees who want to make sure every area of the business is stage ready every single day! When your monthly results statement or profit and loss statement comes in, you are confident as a leader that you and everyone on your store roster plays a role in being stage ready. As the top leader, your expectations have to be crystal clear. When your team gets it right, commend them; when it is wrong, address the behavior that impacted the stage experience negatively. Accountability for delivering a stage-ready presentation is a must. In today's competitive retail landscape, you can't afford for those customers who shop you to feel as though you are average; they can get average anywhere. Create an experience that is something to see. That is why you and your team are onstage in a glass house where your performance is observed daily from all angles. Being stage ready not just for corporate visits but as a culture in your location will play a significant role in your reputation as a leader, as well as providing career-growth opportunities in the future internally and externally (many great job offers or recruiting offers come from what is visually seen from competition). The takeaway from this chapter is that you are onstage. Be stage ready every single day!

2

BE BRILLIANT IN RETAIL AGILITY

Retail agility is necessary and essential if you desire to be Brilliant in the Basics. As we learned, retail leadership is like a roller-coaster ride: as you approach the car and get strapped in, you are taking a risk that the engineers and attendants have not appropriately prepared the ride. Quick drops, unexpected turns, and fast curves are coming your way as a retail leader, and you will have to be truly agile and capable of maneuvering through this fast-paced career without spiraling in a vortex cycle you can't recuperate from.

Your retail leadership career is much like the exhilarating experience you have while getting strapped into the seat. The trust that you place in your senior leaders to take business risks to move the business forward and your ability to create a vision for your team and execute the plan depend on your ability to exhibit retail agility.

Decisions. Decisions. Decisions. We believe that cliché started with an interview with a retail leader. Just kidding. However, on a day-to-day basis, you will receive simultaneous directions from the corporate office, your supervisor, and your customers. You must possess the characteristics that showcase your brilliance in being agile and capable of turning on a dime to achieve the desired outcome or goal. As a retail leader, you can't take it personally and hold on to yesterday's direction with so much passion that you cannot accept change or change management. Company initiatives change to stay relevant and ahead of the competition.

You have to be a change agent and embrace change; change is inevitable in retail. Be prepared to have a compelling point of view in regard to company change. Push back respectfully where you see fit based on facts from your customers or team that the senior leadership might need to know, but keep in mind the big picture and where the company is trying to take the organization. Remember, you are onstage, as mentioned earlier, so that means your team and line-level employees are watching your behavior and demeanor toward the change you are leading. You are the representative of the company brand.

When you think of retail agility, you may ponder personal questions that come to mind, such as all the chaos and multiple decisions you have to deal with on a day-to-day basis:

- When will I get promoted?
- Why do I always get overlooked?
- What more do they want from me?

If you have asked yourself these questions, it may be because you aren't stretching yourself. Leaders who inspire to do more are naturally agile. They can multitask, take on additional assignments, and work extremely well under timeline constraints. If you find yourself being frustrated at having to juggle multiple tasks, you may have to focus on the Three Ds: **Do It, Delegate It, or Destroy It**.

DO IT, DELEGATE IT, OR DESTROY IT

Prioritize. If it's something that absolutely requires your attention; then you will have to DO IT. If you can DELEGATE, then **Inspect What You Expect**, and assign it to someone; it will make you more agile. If you simply needed to be informed about a task, then read and DESTROY the information. Only you can decide which complex issues you are juggling fall into each category. An agile leader will have the ability in their business rhythm to take on something extra and still be successful without showing outer signs of stress or frustrations.

If you ever visit the state of Louisiana, you may stumble upon the locals using the word "lagniappe." It simply means a little something extra. In the retail landscape, your employer and your customers will appreciate when you give them a little something extra, or more than they expected. This gives you an opportunity to differentiate yourself from others, which leaves a lasting favorable impression. Your character, brand, and reputation will have increased notoriety if you are known for exceeding expectations. Each day, when you walk in your building, glance up at the sign before entering and imagine it is flashing in big bold neon letters "LAGNIAPPE."

What does it really mean to be agile or stretch yourself? There are several ways in which you can show your worth in preparation for your next role. Let's look at a couple that have shown proven success:

1. Ask your boss, "What can I take off of your plate?"

    Every leader is expected to accomplish a certain number of tasks and fulfill various responsibilities. Your boss is no different. His or her job description carries the expectation to be effective in his or her role. When you ask, "What can I do to take something you are working on off of your plate?" be genuine and sincere, but, most importantly, be highly effective in your current role. Your boss cannot take you seriously if you are struggling in your position. You can't take on a stretch assignment if your ship is sinking. Make sure your ship is sailing smoothly and on course first. Then your question to your boss should be most definitely appreciated.

2. Are there special projects the district, market, or division is tasked to achieve that you have the ability to help oversee?

    It could be a segment metric of the business, a training project, or a sales goal of a certain item of the week or month, etc. If you can provide that little something extra, that lagniappe, you will impact the goal in a positive manner. By personally overseeing or taking the lead of a stretch assignment, you can make a positive difference to the organization and your personal brand as a leader. You never know: The stretch assignment(s) you take on that yield great results could be defining moments in your career, separating you from being looked upon as an ordinary leader to an extraordinary leader who has potential to handle much more responsibility within the organization.

Your personal stock goes up and you become more marketable within the organization each time you take a task from strategy to execution! In the staff meetings that you aren't part of, your name will come up in a favorable way because of your leadership agility. Your capacity and skill set make the agenda in the room with decision makers. Every retail organization is looking for leaders who take initiative, connect well with people to achieve an outcome, volunteer, or have the skill set to take on more scope of work without losing sight of their key daily responsibilities. Retail leadership agility will prove vital to your overall success and career path. When you achieve this status or reputation by positioning yourself to be seen as an agile employee with capabilities of handling proficiently whatever task comes your way, you have achieved the emerging leader status in the eyes of those who have the ability to reward you for your performance. Take the time to reflect on what keeps your boss up at night and determine what you can do to take that anxiety off their plate! We just walked you through the potential outcome of you using the "lagniappe" mentality in regard to stretch assignments and your boss!

AGILITY AND SUCCESS

By now it should be obvious that nobody should be more invested in your personal development than you. Make an honest assessment of what you know you need to achieve your goals. Many people strive for promotions without the skills. They approach the retail leader role with the mind-set that "I will fake it until I make it." The trouble with that philosophy is that at some point that truth will come to light! Be on point about keeping yourself abreast of what is going on in your company and business. Retail is an ever changing landscape, and you have to be extremely knowledgeable about your business and business results. There are many retail organizations that have free to low-cost training sessions that can help "keep your saw sharp," so to speak. Take time to research what your company offers in regard to training and certification. that can benefit you in your current and future roles. There may be discounted online college courses to help you achieve that degree, master's, or MBA. This investment of your time can have a great return. Again, agility comes into play. You have to be agile in your work-life balance. If you take on too much at one time, it could be disastrous to your career. Approach your leadership with honesty in regard to your capacity. It has been said that knowledge is power, but it isn't really until it is applied to a situation. Can learning a different language improve your employee and/or customer experience? Could you gain a deeper understanding of monthly profit and loss statements?

Have you spent time with community leaders in the area so that you can gain knowledge that will be mutually beneficial to you and the organization you work for? Do you know something about your competition that gives you a personal edge on achieving your personal goals and store goals by being actively involved in the community? It is a richness that cannot be described with words when we volunteer our time and educate ourselves about the communities we are privileged to serve.

Retail agility will lend also to you capitalizing on career paths that you could be most successful in and being nimble enough to know what is right for you based on your education, experience, and background. Take the time to write down your strengths and areas of deficiency in your leadership. Seek out ways within your control to enhance those areas of opportunities through computer-based learning or higher education. Pace yourself in a way that you achieve the goal you desire. In today's technologically advanced society, the chances are very good that whatever area you feel needs development can be improved with an education program right at the touch of your smart device. Take the time to invest in YOURSELF—don't rely solely on what your past experiences have taught you—to make you successful in the future!

It has been said that "When put in charge, take charge." If you have aspirations to grow within your organization, plan on being flexible and adjustable in your personal thoughts. As a leader, you will have to have the business results to back up your desire to advance. Leaders typically don't reward poor performance. No one should know your business better than you! The retail environment is highly competitive and operates under the umbrella of change management. Your competition is internal and external. Your ability to be an agile leader will have a strong bearing on your success. You have to position your team to deliver consistently good or great results. You need to be in the top performers through "planning your work and working your plan." Make a personal decision that if you are being measured by a metric, you will be glad for that measurement to be shown all the way to the top of the organization. Leaders lead, which means you have to be great at knowing when to delegate and when not to.

Inspect what you expect, or your results will always be lacking. If it is important to you as the leader, it will be important to your team. You alone shouldn't feel all of the pressure to deliver great results; it is a shared healthy anxiety to meet and exceed expectations daily. Those you are privileged to lead should feel that same obligation to deliver world-class results. Your team should be enabled and obligated to perform at a high level each day they come to work! If those you lead don't feel a level of responsibility to deliver outstanding results, there is a terrible miss in communication and expectations. Your stretch assignment in terms of business results is fairly simple:

1. Give clear direction.
2. Gain alignment on the goals and expectations.
3. Get a firm commitment from those you lead on the desired outcome.

These three simple steps will help you in any store, district, market division, or company stretch goals. Just like the roller-coaster analogy, you, as a retail leader, will go through many turns, twists, drops, and unexpected steep curves. Your agile behaviors can differentiate you from your peer group; set a precedent with your team as it pertains to your leadership character in the face of change. To be brilliant in retail, you must become a student of the business! Great business acumen is a requirement of a retail leader to be successful. It should be taught to those you lead to maximize your bottom line profits.

Now that you have the tools to manage though change management and understand the importance of being agile in the ever changing landscape of retail, let's move on to discuss how knowledge can make you Brilliant in retail!

3

BE BRILLIANT IN
RETAIL LEADERSHIP KNOWLEDGE

Have you ever wondered, as you are sorting through those ad papers, how they can afford to offer an item so cheaply? Well, dear friend, those inexpensive, almost unbelievable sale items are called "lost leaders." They are what retailers advertise to get you into the store or into the twenty-first century online shop. As a member of management, it is your responsibility to turn these "unprofitable" items into profitable sales for your company.

In order to accomplish this, you must first be able to analyze and understand your business.

Retail is fun, exciting, and forever changing. No matter the retail industry in which you work, the goal is the same: make money. Each leader is expected to understand how to accomplish this within their respective store, district, or region. I started my selling career with A&W Hot Dogs. At the age of seventeen, I was responsible for opening the food kiosk in the mall, ordering products, taking inventory, and accounting for the sales through the register transactions. If my boss hadn't believed in me, and, more importantly, if I hadn't expressed an interest in knowing our business, our business wouldn't have flourished like it did. When I knew the details behind our operating model and company strategies, I was able to execute on them at a high level because I was brought in to the philosophy due to the clarity in which the message was delivered.

Each employee at every level of the organization is responsible for knowing aspects of the business that are directly related to their job function. Why is it important in a retail environment? Simply said, so you will know how and where to spend your time, energy, and resources. Knowing your business goes beyond knowing your store numbers; it's knowing how your district, region, division, or whole company is performing. Where does your company stand in its respective industry?

BUILDING BUSINESS ACUMEN

As I shared earlier, I was exposed to business acumen early in my retail career. Mind you, I didn't know I would build a career in retail at that time; I was just following the direction of my boss and earning my keep. The foundation that was laid at my first job helped me to achieve success in subsequent positions. This foundation included words like "sales," "profitability," "shrink," "wages," "profit," "loss," and "planograms," just to name a few.

This is just a snapshot of knowing your business. Understanding the language is the first step in knowing your business.

What's the difference between a P&L and a SOS? Nothing but the name; they both refer to operating statements, profit and loss, and store operating statement.

Business acumen is defined as "keenness and quickness in understanding and dealing with a business situation in a manner that is likely to lead to a good outcome." Let's work backward from what we have covered thus far. Examples of good outcome, as referenced in the definition, could be exceeding sales goals, increasing profitability, lowering shrink, managing wages, and creating an environment where employees deliver consistent world-class service.

My first exposure to business acumen was a dot-matrix-printed P&L statement, about one hundred–odd pages, during my very first store manager role. The company in which I worked did not have a culture of inclusion. The only person who was allowed to review the P&L statement was the store manager, so, as the assistant, I didn't gain access until I was promoted. I know what you are thinking, because, trust me, it was the same thing I openly expressed in my early twenties. How am I going to be held accountable for the business if I can't review the results? This is why it's so important to ask questions and ensure that your foundation is solid. The second step in business acumen is building the relationships with those individuals in which you can ask the what, why, and how.

Who you choose to help provide you guidance will be critical in your understanding and advancement. A brilliant retail leader will take the time to ensure that nobody in the organization can speak to your business results in the building you are privileged to oversee better than you! To illustrate, it can be compared to your own bank account: No other person should be able to tell you how much or little you have and where you spent what you deposited better than you, the owner of that account, with your name attached to the statement each month. You can sit down with your banker and reconcile your account, but, ultimately, you have the responsibility to control what is taken out or put in. You, as a retail leader, have to have that same mentality when it comes to being a brilliant, knowledgeable leader! Every line on your profit and loss statement or store operating statement is there for a reason. Be inquisitive and ask questions until you truly understand every line listed. Be aware of what you personally can control on that statement and what you can't! Once you have differentiated what's controllable and what's not, be brilliant at controllable lines on that operating statement. Take personal ownership, as if you owned the business, to know where every dollar is being spent and why. Brilliant owner-operator mentality helps enhance your knowledge about the business and assures your success as a retail leader.

4

BE BRILLIANT IN COMMUNICATION

The ability to communicate effectively is an art; not everyone is able to do it well. Many text books have been designed to help people improve in the area of communication. Many families, business organizations, and even nations have failed because of ineffective communication. If you truly want to work in retail, you have to be successful in effective communication and master it as an art! Every single day in retail, as a leader, you will have to communicate, whether you work at the organization's highest and most powerful position or if you are the entry level leader with your first set of store keys. The amount of formal degrees, letters behind your name, and institutional training does not automatically make you effective in communicating. In fact, many well educated people in prestigious positions often struggle at the art of effective communication. This chapter will be vital in regard to the basics that can assist you in effective communication. Let's discuss some basic things to avoid and some basic strategies to execute every day as a retail leader!

THE SILENT TREATMENT

Oftentimes, I have seen great leaders in retail who, when faced with difficult conversations, avoid communication like the plague and put it off. This style of leadership will never get you the optimal result. The lack of effective communication will only prolong the concerns you have as a leader with the individual or associate in retail, and, eventually, your original concern will fester into a bigger concern because you didn't address it in the first place. The longer you wait, the worse the issue that needs addressing will become. We all have the same 168 hours in a week, but what we do with them is our choice. Delaying an overdue performance conversation will only eat away or cost you more of your precious time in the future. The reality is that the other employees or associates are counting on you to do the right thing and have the conversation. The silent treatment is not an option if you want to be successful in your retail career. Unfortunately, many leaders use this tactic to send a message to the underperformers, thinking, "I will show them; I will just wait until a formal sit down discussion (annual evaluation, mid-year check-in, etc.), and then I will spring it on them like a bad surprise party that went terribly wrong." This choice in communication style is ineffective; you can be assured it will be less productive than giving honest feedback when it is needed.

SITUATIONS, BEHAVIORS, AND IMPACT

To be sure you are communicating effectively, tailor your conversations based on the following: **What's the Situation? What's the Behavior? What's the Impact? (Three Ws)**:

- **Situation**—when communicating effectively, you will describe the situation that you would like to talk to someone about with all clarity. Consider the audience, and tailor your verbiage to them. Don't assume they are knowledgeable or aware of all of the company-abbreviated, standard operating procedures and policies. Be specific, and share the details fully about the situation at hand that warrants discussion.

- **Behavior**—discuss the undesired behavior(s) that you currently see, and then discuss the behavior change you are expecting to see. It would be beneficial to have a copy of their job description handy if warranted so full transparency is available if needed. Like a well recorded event, describe the behaviors you have witnessed (and/or others) with the appropriate dates, times, and places. This technique will also save you time because it minimizes a debate when you recall, just like a video, the concerns that you or others have personally observed.

- **Impact**—describe in depth the impact their behavior is having on the customers, employees, and/or the organization. Help them to see that they are not adding value to the brand or culture/environment conducive to growing the business. Then, be very specific about the desired behaviors you wish to see in order for them to be successful. This type of effective communication will lead you toward the desired outcome you are striving for with the associate or employee.

There is no guarantee you will win over all you practice this method with; however, your chances are better with this approach. Why would I say that? Well, even the written record of the greatest man who ever walked the earth shows he picked an employee who didn't make the grade out of the original twelve disciples. If it could happen with him, it could happen with you as a retail leader. People may demonstrate the right behaviors initially but may need to be replaced after careful observations.

INFLAME, INFORM, OR INSPIRE

As a retail leader, your emotions will get tested daily in all aspects. Whether in written form or verbally, people can **Inflame, Inform, or Inspire**. From the moment you get dressed in the morning and check your smart device, you will skim over a few company e-mails, and then you will start to be impacted emotionally by what you just read. Throughout the day, you will hear many comments, opinions, and complaints that will impact you as well.

I know a retail leader, fairly new to the organization, who was challenged with running a retail store in a challenging demographic market. He was relatively new to the organization. Notice how he used effective communication involving the **Three Is** on his endeavor with the market.

Inflame

The retail leader definitely wanted to avoid inflaming the new team with his communication. This often happens when new leaders make snide comments or comparisons to the former leader or leadership team, trying to build their credibility for themselves.

The employees or associates he had the privilege to lead had a reputation for being difficult, and the performance outcomes were not looked upon favorably. The engagement score taken by a third-party group showed this particular store to be one of the worst in a fleet of about a thousand stores. This retail chain had stores that ranged in annual revenue from approximately $45 million to $100 million per big box. What would this leader need to do to oversee in this Fortune 500 company? According to him, he started with effective communication.

Inform

The leader had the personnel manager print a roster of all of the associates in the building. He then asked for her to help schedule a meeting one-on-one with every associate on the roster. There were approximately 150 employees. One by one, he met with each of them, including the five salary managers who reported to him. On a yellow notepad—the traditional leadership tool—he took notes and asked questions to seek insight.

Here were the questions and format the leader followed:

- What do you expect from me as your general manager?
- What do you expect of the other managers in this building?
- What would make this the greatest place to work on the planet?
- Do you know how the store is doing in performance? Your department? You?
- What ideas can you share with me to make our culture world class and impact our customers' shopping experience in a legendary way?

Inspire

The leader thanked them for their insight and then practiced effective communication by giving clear direction and gaining alignment on policies, goals, and standards. Once that had been achieved, he asked for their commitment and gave them his.

In closing, he said, "I have your insights written down, and I would like to share my direction":

- Every customer within ten feet deserves a hello.
- Any spills or trash on the ground should be cleaned up so our reputation is never tarnished.
- Every associate has an idea or opinion that will be embraced.
- A suggestion box will be kept outside the office; please share your thoughts, and we will examine what's in the box weekly at our leadership meeting.
- Please read over your job description, give me your best every day you come to work, and I will commend you for it daily.

- Make sure before you leave that you come say good bye, and I will do the same. I want to ensure that you had a great day here.

You have a choice as you start your day how you will allow others to have an impact on your communication style. Stop and make a wise decision because you, as a retail leader, never want to damage your brand or career out of emotion. Reflect on those beautiful pictures of your family and vacations on your desk at work and just how much your family and employment mean to you! Never allow someone or something to have the power to change you to become out of character or someone else. When you reply to the e-mails you have read with effective communication, you need to keep in mind, "Will this e-mail inflame, inform, or inspire the receiver of my e-mail?" I often say that the key "send" is not your friend! With this approach, you will never have regrets about what you just said. The thing about e-mails is that they provide an electronic paper trail and can be held forever. You never know who will eventually end up with the e-mail you just sent. An effective communicator is cognizant of the **Three Is** at all times! Once you arrive at your building, effective communication should kick in at high gear. Always let your team see you at your very best, just like the Disney characters previously discussed. You have the same mentality as a retail leader; be in character from the moment you walk in your building, and your emotions and communication style as the leader will have a direct impact on your day. People often say, "People First and Profits Will Follow." There is a lot of truth to that statement; putting people first in business and life will make a world of difference in yours. Just like e-mail, your verbal words will do the same thing as the **Three Is.**

SMART

Engaged associates or employees have the biggest impact on your organizational goals; in short, bet on your people. It's the most precious asset you have on the job! The key to success is finding the recipe to inspire engagement through effective communication. It is pretty simple but often missed by leaders in retail because they are more focused on the bottom line or P&L every month than effective communication to the people that got them the results on that profit and loss statement. You will often see key leaders in high retail positions have knee-jerk reactions when financial results come out and then have emergency conference calls to discuss the horrific results instead of an effective plan of communication. They inadvertently choose to inflame already disengaged leaders to become even more disengaged on a call or WebEx by reiterating how horrible the results are in the division, region, district, or their store. News flash: This type of communication is toxic and contagious. There will be a negative ripple effect that takes place in an organization at lightning speed with this style of communication. This ineffective communication style will grow legs and cascade to everyone in the building, causing chaos, turnover, and turmoil instead of inspiration and behavior changes. You have to choose to filter this information from your leader if this takes place and communicate effectively to those you lead. You have the ability as a retail leader to make a difference; in all actuality, you are obligated to do so once you take on a leadership role. Never "third-party" manage or meet with your team by saying, "They said we need to . . ." This is somewhat a sign of lack of confidence, passing the buck and leadership ownership. You are responsible to deliver the filtered message as if it were your own! When put in charge, take charge! You are the leader. Interact with your team daily; choose your effective communication verbiage wisely, and it won't cast a negative light on those you report to for the organization. Use your effective communication skill to influence without authority when the occasion arises to do so. You can be instrumental with effective communication in influencing people and changing behaviors. The by-product of your choice of communicating effectively will be a better P&L, or bottom line result!

Instead of waiting by the smart device and computer screen to view the results of the P&L each month, what if retail leaders anxiously looked for those results, not just for the bottom line but for framing the conversation up to get those people together who delivered the result and have them help create SMART action plans? SMART stands for **Specific, Measurable, Attainable, Realistic, and Timely**. Together, these components can be used to correct deficiencies and shortcomings as a team. This, dear friend, would be being brilliant in the basics in regard to communication. Don't underestimate your people; the answer is always in the room. They are truly at ground zero where the rubber meets the road. Give clear directions, get alignment and commitment, and great things can happen in the retail business. The only way to get that answer in the room is with effective communication from you as the retail leader!

THE FOLLOW-UP ALIGNMENT

Let's return to the above retail leader example. After meeting with every associate, there were basics that were aligned on as a team. The leader gave the salary managers an additional point or two, which consisted of taking twenty minutes of their day saying hello to every associate in the building. This was called "Take 20." It was a simple hello, nothing about business. He wanted them to just share a genuine greeting. The first time a leader's face was seen every day, it was pleasant, enthusiastic, and non-business-related. Once the rounds of the entire store were made, then they could come back and give direction; feedback on performance, department look and feel; and all around normal coaching, just by walking around. None of this took place until after the "Take 20" was complete every single day!

THE FOLLOW-UP COMMITMENT

This process or cadence went on for months; before the store realized what happened, the culture became sustainable, and management was using effective communication. All the stakeholders in the building were able to build teams that produced results through effective communication and utilization of employee and customer insight.

Every single associate in the building could speak with clarity to the financial acumen, daily business plan or state budget sales, profit goals, and expectations of them in their role. If you were to be present at the morning meetings or team huddles, you couldn't tell who was the newest employee and who was the general manager because every associate was trained and developed to understand basic business acumen. They knew the store budget goals and how they contributed on their shift to meet the goals through legendary service and commitment to not misspeaking to one single customer who took the time to come in and support the store because they had a choice in where to shop. They knew that each dollar spent by that customer contributed to their paycheck and livelihood and that this was a noncommission retailer. Effective communication was alive and well because the morning shift would communicate with the evening shift on where they were in sales, traffic count, profit margin, and what was left to achieve in regard to budget through great customer interactions on their shift.

One year later, when the survey results came out surrounding associate engagement, this leader, his leadership team, and, most importantly, the associates and employees had changed the culture 180 degrees and had taken the survey results to one of the top engagement stores in the entire company with profits to match. What a celebration they had—a total store meeting where every single associate was recognized for their personal contribution. They couldn't have champagne, but they enjoyed some nice sparkling cider in really nice glasses.

The moral to the story is that clear communication is effective when it encompasses direction, alignment, and commitment. These factors will yield great results in retail leadership.

How can I be so confident? I was that leader who had the privilege to witness the transformation through effective communication! I proudly display the glass hardware trophy in my office from an incredible team I will never forget from Houston, Texas! Your career in retail can be so rewarding with fond memories of great people and teams. You will work for all types of leaders; some you will remember for the greatness they inspired you to do, and some you will just plain remember. They may have led through intimidation, had emotional outbursts, or were even unfit to be leaders. However, you still can learn from them. It is called "what not to do" as a leader. Practice being cool, calm, and collected because your team is watching your every move and they are counting on your professionalism and leadership to shine through. When you have those announced or unannounced visits from leaders north of you in rank, don't make excuses about the areas of concern. You are the leader . . . Lead! Have a sense of urgency to correct the concerns and use the opportunity to teach and train your team to raise the bar to deliver better results. Your ability to communicate effectively will come into play in moments just like those described. The outcome you are seeking will be through clear direction, alignment, and commitment. If you fail at this, so will your team!

Ultimately, your success will be determined by many factors; however, effective communication is a key component of the many other factors. Communicating to each generation in a way that is meaningful to them will be very important. You should take the time to research methods that will show success. There is richness to diversity and inclusion, and those leaders and organizations that figure out how to communicate and embrace them effectively will have an advantage in today's retail sector.

The premise of this book is to help you see that by being brilliant in the basics you can elevate your leadership and impact the lives of those who work for and with you on a daily basis. You may be thinking, "I can't afford the time to talk to every associate about their role, schedule leaders to just to walk around and say hello the first twenty minutes of every day, or read associates' ideas and customers' insight weekly out of suggestion boxes." My question to you is, "As a current retail leader or potential retail leader, can you afford not to?" Remember, we all have the same 168 hours in a week; as a retail leader, you have to decide what is most important to you and where you can invest your time that will give you the greatest return! Your victories as a retail leader will always trace back to a foundation of being effective in communication.

5

BE BRILLIANT IN
PERSONAL ACCOUNTABILITY

In today's retail environment, I feel no word is referenced more often in relation to performance than "accountable." You will hear phrases like "He or She needs to be held accountable," or "When you get that promotion you desired, a conversation comes along with it that starts with 'You are accountable for . . .'" A great way to think about accountability is to compare it to your personal credit rating; ultimately, you are accountable for the score based off of your ability to be responsible for the decisions you personally make every day in regard to your credit. In retail, accountability is huge in making you as a leader have a strong brand and credibility and achieve the organization's results. You, dear friend, are on the proverbial hook! Often, in a retail leadership role, you will find yourself at some point in your career coming up short in some metric or goal on your profit and loss statement. In your mind, you could feel you have exhausted all avenues and find yourself scratching your head and saying every month that passes, "I don't see the needed improvement in this certain area of my business." Guess what? Your boss, or direct report, is looking at the same profit and loss statement and doesn't see the needed improvement either. The definition of insanity, as you already know, is doing the same thing over and over again and expecting a different outcome magically on your profit and loss statement (commonly known as the P&L). Herein lies the introduction of the chapter five theme: personal accountability. In retail, underperformance will eventually get you a poor evaluation, loss of credibility, lack of respect from your peers, or, with consistent documentation, a promotion to customer!

ACCOUNTABILITY PARTNERS

Having an accountability partner can help keep you on track and making good decisions that help you avoid the stress of what I just mentioned. An accountability partner can be internal or external to your organization; however, they need to be knowledgeable, educated in your field, and able to have access to discuss your results as a roadmap to how you're trending or tracking toward your goal. Your accountability partner also needs to have the intestinal fortitude to be forthright and honest with you to keep you on track to achieve the desired result. In my thirty plus years of retail, the most effective leaders were open to feedback and truly embraced constructive criticism. An accountability partner is mutually beneficial because a mutual relationship allows a fresh set of eyes to examine your work while you do the same for your partner. You both benefit from the wisdom and knowledge of the other.

Commendation is due when you are on track; honest direct feedback is due to you when you aren't.

For example, imagine your retail store is missing the goal in "shrink" (or budgeted loss profits). You truly are struggling to put your finger on the reason for the profit/loss underperformance in the building, but your P&L continues to show it is an opportunity under your leadership. You could continue the death spiral in this category of poor performance, or you could recognize you need an accountability partner to come walk your building and provide advice that could save you from the dismal outcome of doing the same things that are getting you the current result! Your accountability partner might look at the key categories in your building and drill down to a root cause analysis. They might also highlight areas of the company-provided standard operating policies or procedures that your building is currently not executing in accordance with those compliance polices. Together, you can think strategically and develop a roadmap to success with specific check-in points along the way to guarantee a different outcome than high shrink and low performance results. The plan you and your accountability partner develop could center on shared best practices, as well as tough or critical conversations that must take place with key leaders or stakeholders in your building who you lead, with specific deadlines. You could create a SMART action plan:

- Specific
- Measurable
- Attainable
- Realistic
- Timely

This is where the value of an accountability partner really comes into play; you won't be able to procrastinate or put off the role or ownership you have in changing the results because your accountability partner will do just that—hold you accountable! In turn, you could provide the same service to your accountability partner in some metric in their business. The richness of this process is in two people truly looking out for the best interest in your career! The on-point feedback and direction is priceless as a leader in retail! Find the right accountability partner who will devote the time to be great at this role, and you have struck gold!

ACCOUNTABILITY PARTNER CHARACTERISTICS

What characteristics would you look for in a great accountability partner? Here are just a few:

- Trustworthiness—doesn't over promise and under deliver
- Knowledge—has advance knowledge of the subject they are peering into with you
- Vested Interest in Your Success—truly practices the golden rule of more happiness in giving than receiving, believes in you as a leader, and wants to see you succeed
- Dependability—reliable and able to give you constructive feedback, seasoned the right way to be palatable when served up to you to digest

- Punctuality or Timeliness in Feedback—sets specific dates to discuss the data or analytics and your improvement in the key categories of concern

These key characteristics are just a few qualities you should ponder when determining how to select an accountability partner. To illustrate the power of selecting the right accountability partner to move performance in positive way, I would like to use a personal example. A few months ago, I was given a wonderful gift—let's call it an "Itbit"—by someone who has a vested interest in my health, well-being, and life longevity. I was hesitant at first to wear it, let alone take the time to charge it, to sync it to my phone, and to review my daily step activity, calories burned, sleep pattern, and steps climbed. In a course of time, after establishing a cadence of wearing this gift at the right time, my healthy life accountability partner encouraged me to sign up for a group challenge or "work week hustle." It amounted to about ten people having a line of sight to all of your steps daily and then force ranking the individual performance daily. Everyone would know if you were doing well in steps taken or if your performance needed drastic improvement within the team of challengers. The first day of the challenge, I caught myself for the first time in my life concerned about the number of steps I had taken in a day. Never before had I noticed or even cared about this data. It truly was irrelevant to me; however, now that I knew how many I had taken, my bigger concern was how my performance compared to the others in the work week challenge. I found myself taking conference calls with ear buds so I could walk and talk at the same time in order to stay aligned or ahead of the group. At the end of my work day, although often tired, I would find the motivation to go get in two to three more miles simply because I had an accountability partner who had a vested interest in me watching my every step—literally. That vested interest, by the end of the week, inspired me to achieve well over one hundred thousand steps in five days and take the number-one spot, which never would have been achieved without the support of my life accountability partner! If you achieve your goals, metrics, and career aspirations in retail, it will be with the support of you finding, appreciating, and utilizing your personal accountability partner. So if you think you want to be in retail as a leader, acquire and hold on to a great accountability partner!

6

BE BRILLIANT IN NETWORKING

NETWORKING

Networking is the most underutilized tool in any retail manager's toolbox. Your ability to have open networks could be compared to getting off at five o'clock in a large metropolitan city and traveling on the interstate in rush-hour traffic. If you had a passenger, you could expedite your trip by utilizing the HOV lane (high occupancy vehicle lane) and zoom right by the congestion. In retail, your ability to build strong open networks that are diverse and deep could put you, my friend, in the retail HOV lane in regards to your career. Many great leaders with awesome accomplishments will miss out on significant opportunities because of not leveraging their networks.

When you leverage your networks, you will lead more effectively and achieve organizational and personal goals and objectives with speed!

When is the last time you truly looked through your smartphone and analyzed what your personal network looked like? How often do you call the top twenty on your call list, and how often do they impact your business results? Are they in the same genre as you? There is a tremendous value in the retail industry as a leader when you take a self-examination on this topic and have an honest assessment of the following:

IS MY NETWORK CLOSED OR OPEN?

A closed network consists of a group of individuals in the same business unit or segment. They will have similar beliefs, projects, experience, backgrounds, and education. A closed network is useful but doesn't serve at the same weight or capacity as an open network.

A closed network fails to adapt to new situations (which happen often in retail), causes you to miss out on job opportunities and career growth, minimizes your ability to leverage influence, and puts you in a situation of often utilizing groupthink based on everyone having the same line of thought!

An open network would consist of various business unit segments that have a richness in diversity of thought, background, experience, and education. For example, in the typical structure of an organization, there would exist a CEO, VP of operations, HR, project teams, legal, safety, warehousing or distribution centers, administration, payroll, compensation, etc., etc. A person who had an open network would have built relationships with people in all these different disciplines or segments. With those connections, they are able to make faster and more accurate decisions than someone who only had connections or networks in one part of the business, such as payroll!

It should should start to click now that, to be agile and nimble and move with speed in the fast-paced retail environment, which typically moves at the speed of light, you must have strong open networks to be highly successful in your role. Without them, your e-mails for assistance could wind up in the age-old "unread" or "deleted" file! No doubt this tool in your toolbox could heighten your credibility and notoriety for getting things done as a retail leader!

Open networks foster group innovation and career mobility and adapt to changing environments, and your ability to influence is maximized as a result!

Strong effective networks will have the following as a common theme:

- Bidirectional—connected at various levels of the organization, not just your peer group or discipline
- Mutually Beneficial
- Give-and-Take Relationships
- Trust, Commitment

- Expected Responsiveness
- Self-Disclosure
- Ongoing Interaction
- Frequent Contact (six months or less)

HOW DIVERSE IS MY NETWORK?

When you truly understand networking, you will seek a variety of individuals that are different from you in all shapes, forms, and fashions. Experience is so impactful to retail leaders; having access to diversity of thought, culture, ethnicity, background, and education will put you at the top of the retail leaders list! As our society continues to become more diverse, our approach to retail should as well. Great companies and leaders know to surround themselves with generational differences and all of the above previously mentioned, and they gain a wealth of insight from those who will keep their business performance strong. Imagine you worked in the organization structure I referenced earlier. If you could gain assistance through your network with legal, HR, the warehouse, and payroll within a few quick calls or e-mails, you just gave power to your most precious asset . . . Time! Others may take days, weeks, or months to accomplish what you did in just minutes because of the diverse network you had built. When you picked up the phone, your contact answered with an attitude of, "What can I do to help or support you?" because of your relationships in diverse areas of the business, not just with your current role peers. Many leaders have leaped past the masses by having focus groups with diverse groups or individuals to gain insight on how to merchandise, hire, and create a culture in their retail environment that matches the needs of those who shop their organization, all accomplished through diverse networking! Put this advice on the top of your to-accomplish list! Watch the impact to your bottom line, and notice how you differentiate your retail leadership from others who don't get it or don't want to get it! Our own unconscious bias can be a retail career killer.

Diverse networks are connections that cross critical boundaries in the organization. They require relationships with mutually beneficial partnerships vertically and horizontally within the organizational structure of your retailer.

HOW DEEP IS YOUR NETWORK?

Deep networks are quality relationships with others from different backgrounds with whom you exchange information, resources, and skills. These deep networks of relationships provide valuable perspectives and resources including social support and camaraderie in the workplace .

A deep network consists of people who will go the extra mile for you because of the relationship they have with you that was built over time! These are your go-to people who have strong ties with you and the organization. They keep you informed ahead of time about future changes, events, and business moves you should contemplate. They give you insight in advance about others in your peer group because of the trust between you: a deep network that is mutually beneficial! It can't be a relationship that is deep if it is one sided, in which you receive but never share. As a retail leader, look for ways to establish networks in your organization that will be deep and mutually beneficial. It will propel you to the top of the peer group!

After self-reflection and analysis of your personal network, ask the following questions:

- Is my current network helping me with challenges in my current role?
- In what ways is it helping or hindering me?
- What is missing in my network?
- Which relationships are strong?
- Which relationships should I improve?

It has been said, "It's not what you know but who you know." There is so much truth to that age-old statement.

WHO YOU KNOW MATTERS

Have you ever wondered how some leaders in retail seem to always know what is about to change before anyone else? News flash: It is because of their network (or they are just nosy).

Strong, open, diverse, and deep networks can impact your career in various ways. For example, they can inform you about positions that are possibly coming open, buying decisions that impact your bottom line on products that are new or about to be extinct, transforming new leadership structure or who is about to be replaced, etc., etc. The list can go on and on. The depth of your network can truly impact your personal career, and it most definitely depends on who you know. You can't pick your family, but you can pick your network!

Take a network analysis of yourself: write down twenty people who are important to you in your professional network. They can be people who provide you information and resources, help you solve complex problems at work, or provide you with developmental advice or personal support. They can exist inside or outside your current organization.

After writing your names down (probably the first time in your life for this exercise), then examine the list to see if it is open or closed, as mentioned earlier.

Is it diverse, with differences that are rich in culture, generational thought, background, education, ethnicity and experience?

If your overall answers are yes, then congratulations on having an open network that is extremely useful in being successful in retail leadership!

Your open network will take you a long way in your career but there is another aspect to retail leadership that is just as important to your ability to effectively network. It actually serves as direct compliment to your network, like parsley on a beautiful balanced entree meal.

YOUR BRAND

Your brand is crucial when it comes to networking. Your reputation gets to the interview room way before you do in your very best suit or dress! Be cognizant in retail as to whom you group yourself with. Do you find you spend your time with the can-do associates or employees or with the ones who always see the glass half empty and see no way out? They constantly are negative and have a dismal view on the job, the leaders, the company direction and especially their career! Your brand, like networking, will put you in the HOV lane or in traffic that could bring your career to a screeching halt! Oftentimes, our brand can be extremely strong at different phases in our career, but then it gets tarnished, and it is extremely hard to clean it up within the same organization. Oftentimes, a person can never overcome the damage done to their brand. Think about people or organizations that you admired or were admired in the public eye, but in an instant they lost the credibility of their brand. Think of the impact it had on them and those who admired them. Wake up every day with the mind-set, "I plan to add value or make deposits today in regards to my brand!" It is most definitely a choice, and it is in your hands to impact every day! We make so many decisions as a retail leader almost every minute of our shift. Never let some scorecard of temporary recognition cause you to compromise your brand for a temporary celebration of being the best in some category of your business if it wasn't accomplished with integrity! Honesty can be defined as what you do when everyone is watching; integrity can be defined as what you do when nobody is around. One of my mentors told me this, and it resonates daily: "Trust, but validate." When it comes to company contests, metrics you measure for results, etc., trust, but validate that the win is clean. Once you validate it personally, then celebrate like crazy! Like an ATM machine, you can only get out of your brand what you personally put in!

Use your network wisely. Unfriend those on the job (like on Facebook) if they do not add value to your current goals in your career but take away from your retail leadership reputation!

SUMMARIZING NETWORKING

From a network perspective in retail, you need these three in your toolbox especially:

1. A Mentor—someone who will shoot straight. They will listen to you vent and express your woes and struggles on the job or at home. They solely have your best interest at heart and will talk you off the retail ledge when you see the dismal no-way-out sign fast

approaching! You can be yourself at all times with this person.

2. An Advisor—someone in your network that gives you solid advice on the career path you are in or are pursuing for future growth. They have been there and done that, so to speak, and are looked upon as successful by others and by you. They are trustworthy and have developed others through experience, background, and education.

3. An Advocate—you have to have an advocate in your network. This person should only see and know of your best behavior! You have to go to them in person and ask them to be your advocate in the retail organization you are in currently. One thing is for sure, my retail leader friends: you will never be in the room when someone is discussing you for a promotion, salary change, or company restructuring. You need an advocate who will speak positively on your behalf when you aren't in

the room. Because they are in your network, don't be afraid to ask them, "What will you say about me?" You want an advocate that will pound the desk on your behalf and state, "You have to promote this person, and here is why. . ."

These three people in your retail network will have the greatest impact on where your career goes in retail! However, nobody should invest in you more than you!

There was once a VP in a small retail company. He had worked for many years for this company and finally made it to a premier spot that had not been occupied by a leader like him before in the history of the company. He started at the very entry-level position of bagging groceries and found himself—years later—as an executive in a two-bil-lion-dollar company. All his evaluation ratings had been "meets" or "exceeds expectations." He was sent by this company to an event where he was able to listen to a key-note speaker from a Fortune 500 company. This person had the title of chief diversity officer in the world's largest retail company. She gave a most inspirational, compelling keynote address about her company and the importance of companies staying relevant by embracing diversity and inclusion. She made the point, "Diversity could be considered being invited to the dance, however, inclusion would be defined as actually dancing!" She made a profound statement that the census shows that minorities are soon to become the majority, so retailers better embrace diverse thought, education, background, ethnicity, gender, etc. to remain relevant in the forthcoming retail sector! The VP of the smaller company found himself sitting at the same table as the chief diversity officer once she concluded her keynote address at this large Southwest conference in Dallas, Texas. He thought to himself, *What are the chances that you get assigned a seat at the table of the keynote speaker of the world's largest retailer?* He pondered, *I can sit here and finish the conference with great notes, or I can introduce myself, exchange business cards, and get to know this inspirational leader in retail through networking.* After just a few minutes of pondering the thought to muster up the boldness to network, he pulled out his business card and, with a grand smile, said hello and shook hands. They exchanged cards and connected on a work-related social media site. They stayed in constant contact long after the conference. One day while the chief diversity officer was traveling abroad, her phone rang, and it was the VP from the smaller company. He was looking for an opportunity because his company had decided to let his talent go after years of dedicated service.This company had a history of this type of behavior. How did networking come into play with its muscle? The chief diversity officer made a few phone calls, and what had seemed dismal became an opportunity to have a career with the world's largest retailer and oversee fifteen states instead of fourteen stores in an East Texas small town with minimal career-growth opportunities. The power of networking is an amazing tool, and it works! How can I be so confident, you may ask? I was the VP!

Let's go to the next chapter and continue our retail leadership ride.

7

BE BRILLIANT IN JOB READINESS

There is not a day that goes by that someone some-where is not anxiously awaiting an upcoming in-terview. Many thoughts go through their head: What suit will I wear? What dress or tie screams, "Pick me"? Have I prepared well enough? Do I have the best back-ground, experience, education, and, in some cases, credit rating to obtain this job? They see themselves in their mind's eye getting that handshake or phone call saying,

"Congratulations; you were our top candidate." In this chapter, we want to discuss some basic things you can be brilliant at to position yourself to be the candidate who gets that handshake or phone call!

The question is, "What will differentiate you from all others applying for the same role?" The truth is that, in most cases, your reputation will arrive long before you do if the retail organization has done its homework. Have your character be your calling card before you get in the room or on the call. When they research you, give them something great to find!

DO YOUR HOMEWORK

In today's modern world, social media and technology allow you, at the touch of a few buttons, to gather great insight that can be extremely beneficial to you prior to the interview. You can usually find the hiring manager on business sites like LinkedIn. Review their background and experience so you can seek out common ground that could make great introductory commentary at the beginning of the interview.

The additional time you took to learn more about the interviewer or the interview panel might lead to great dialogue that could play to your advantage before the notepads even come out.

Once you find interest in a role in retail, dig deeper: Look for insight on who you know that currently holds that role that you are applying for within your network. If they don't exist, find someone who has the same title in that organization or another, and ask detailed questions about what they do and how they get it done successfully. Seek out the names of those considered to be great in the role or subject matter experts. This will help you be prepared for the interview.

Next, read and ponder over the job description to gain clarity on what the company is saying are the basic minimum characteristics they are looking for in the top candidate. Using keywords, they will describe the basic functions of the role in the position that they are seeking to fill. After thoroughly reading and understanding the description, you will know if it is a fit that aligns with your leadership skillset. If it does and you are in a position to take the role on, be ready to relocate, knowing there is minimal risk based on your readiness to perform at a high level in the position. Then, go for it with gusto! Be the candidate who gets that role!

RESUMES

Resumes that will increase your chances of truly being the candidate of choice could be classified as "eye catchers." Simply stated, being brilliant in the basics of resume writing that would catch a hiring manager's eye gives you a distinct chance to land the job you are looking for in retail. Often in retail leadership, resume writing presents a challenge because many retail leaders very rarely have to build an eye-catching resume (if they have one at all). This chapter will assist you in that regard on your journey of being the candidate. Your resume is basically a marketing tool for you! It is a chance for you to broadcast your accomplishments and put forth a positive profile of yourself on paper. It increases your chance to be considered for the role. It differentiates you from others applying for the position. It shows your level of professionalism. By no means is your resume an all-out guarantee that you will get the job or even be interviewed. Your resume should be considered successful if it doesn't exclude you from being considered for the position that you are seeking! Remember this important thing when building a resume that sets you apart and best highlights your work experience and skills: it's not only about you!

Any hiring manager that considers your resume is looking for the answer to the following question: How can this person help me be successful in my role?

Building an eye-catching resume would consist of the following components:

- Contact information—full name, address, telephone numbers, and e-mail.
- Education and certifications—names of schools attended, relevant programs, degrees, certifications, and extra-curricular activities.

- Employment history—work experience, dates of employment, names of employers, titles, job descriptions or duties.
- Skills—mastery-level skills of computer-based processes (Microsoft Excel, WORD, etc.); team building; project oversight.

Provide contact information first. Your e-mail address should be professional and include your name. This address should be a personal address, not a student or company address. Many job seekers use a separate e-mail address reserved specifically for job seeking. Build out your objective statement or summary at the top of your resume, after your contact information. Define your career goals and honestly assess your qualifications. Describe how your unique experience and skills can benefit you and your future direct report. A career summary should quickly communicate who you are as a professional, summarize your greatest strength(s), and convince your hiring manager to feel compelled to keep reading.

There are basically three types of resumes:

- **Functional**—focuses on skills vs. work history.
- **Chronological**—lists job experience that would align with the desired role you are seeking. This resume format is best used to highlight a series of positions that correspond to some part of the same industry or field.
- **Targeted/Combined**—used to put emphasis on specific job skills listing those skills and experiences related to the desired role before discussing employment history. This approach allows you as an applicant to highlight impressive skills and work-related experiences that showcase the alignment with the role you desire. The hiring manager will have a clearer understanding of your solid strengths and interest in the position.

Do's to be brilliant in the basics of building a resume to be the selected or winning candidate:

- ✓ Keep your resume to between one and two pages in length
- ✓ Review grammatical errors
- ✓ Have someone in your network review your resume
- ✓ Be consistent in your spacing and formatting
- ✓ Leave white space; if crowded, it could be difficult to read
- ✓ Use short bullet-pointed sentences to increase ease of reading
- ✓ Include contact information on all pages
- ✓ Be sure that your e-mail address, voicemail message, and social media sites are professional and represent you in a favorable, professional way
- ✓ Use action verbs to provide eye-catching stamina (initiated, supervised, delegated, developed, etc.)

✓ Include volunteer experience

Don'ts in the basics of building your resume:

✓ Strain the hiring manager's eye with font smaller than 10
✓ Use fancy fonts that may be distracting and hard to read
✓ Use large fonts; they may appear humorous
✓ Include salary requirements
✓ Include diversity information; this is irrelevant to the job
✓ Include a photograph; a picture says nothing about your ability to be successful
✓ Include early background; refrain from telling information about your early childhood and upbringing
✓ List hobbies and interests
✓ Mention availability; leave this topic to be discussed in the actual interview

INTERVIEWS

Most candidates will not take the time to do research about the position they are applying for; they simply focus on the title and salary. Those candidates rarely get the handshake or call, but they will often complain that the interview process was unfair or biased. However, in some cases, it was their lack of preparation. Anything in life worth obtaining takes effort. You be the candidate who puts forth effort. Write down your qualities that stand out like your "super powers," so to speak. Think in terms of what things you are really good at that should be discussed in the interview that align with key words in the job description. Strive to make sure those strengths come up, and speak with enthusiasm when they do. A suggestion would be to take the time to plan out a 30/60/90-day plan after researching the role and organization needs. Be specific in what your approach would be if given the opportunity in the first 30 days (usually observation and relationship-building time), 60 days (usually identification of key stakeholders, their gathered insight, and shared vision), 90 days (strategies in place, along with a SMART action plan to impact the business unit positively with future check-ins to validate that you are tracking to achieve the goals). When these type of plans are crafted well in PowerPoint or WORD, they send a loud message to those interviewing you that you went the extra step to differentiate yourself with a plan or strategy already in place if you were announced as the candidate of choice! This shows confidence in yourself and that you possess futuristic-thinking qualities. In retail, that is a plus because it is fast paced and always changing; leaders need to be nimble and agile (always thinking out a quarter, two quarters, three quarters, or a year ahead)! This single act of developing a 30/60/90-day plan will move your interview impression north compared to those who walk in with nothing. If it is a phone interview, send your 30/60/90-day plan to the hiring manager prior to your interview, and it will still have the same positive impact. Just make sure you have researched your data so your plan aligns with the business unit and what the hiring manager is trying to achieve!

To be brilliant in an interview, consider these suggestions:

- Be on time (arrive approximately fifteen minutes early); allow for traffic, construction, or any other unforeseen occurrence that could potentially cause your first impression to be negatively impacted.

- Don't arrive too early and put the interviewer in an unfavorable position to feel obligated to see you sooner than scheduled.

- Dress for success. (Need I say more?) If you desire a professional, responsible position that pays well, then dress like you already have the job. Professional attire has a way of saying you will be getting the right person if you choose me, before you ever say a word!

- Smile and have a firm handshake at the onset, with great eye contact throughout the interview that is appropriate.

- Don't take control of the interview. When the interviewer asks you to talk about yourself or what you have done, be brief and to the point. Don't ramble on and on and find yourself talking for a third of the allotted interview time about your background. Remember, the interviewer is intelligent enough to read your application or resume that has your background information; they are listening for your brief statement for compelling and interesting information that is deeper than what is on your resume paper.

- Prepare situation, behavior, and outcome success stories from your past in your mind so that you can speak with clarity.

- If salary comes up, think through what is commensurate for the job description and consider that in your reply.

- Leave with another firm handshake, and say thank you!

- Send a thank you e-mail to the person who interviewed you within twenty-four hours of the interview.

8

BE BRILLIANT IN MODELING SERVANT-LEADER CHARACTER

As a leader in any organization, your character is on display 24/7. Your newest employee to your most seasoned employee is watching your style of leadership from the moment you walk in your building (along with your customers). Perform as if you have the CEO sitting on your shoulder watching every single decision you make all day. If you maintain this mentality, you will most likely do the right things to represent yourself and the company brand favorably and to retain your customer loyalty. Character is something you make deposits on daily. Many have spent a lifetime making deposits, but, in one single instance, they make a withdrawal and it ruins them, their brand image, and their company for life. I will mention a few names and what comes to mind: Enron, Lance Armstrong, OJ Simpson. If I were a betting person—and I'm not—I'd bet you probably didn't think about the good things Enron did for the community, the excellent speed and riding style of Lance Armstrong, or the victories of the Buffalo Bills when OJ played running back with #32 on his jersey. You see, our minds are wired to remember their character flaws when they all fell from grace. The lesson we can all take away as retail leaders is "Don't find yourself making a withdrawal of that magnitude that sends your career in a death spiral, along with your personal brand and reputation." You will be challenged to meet metrics, business goals, and strategies as a retail leader. *Never* compromise your integrity for a momentary win on a company scorecard or to be momentarily celebrated as a winner. A lie can only live until the truth catches up to it. Avoid the stress of wondering if today is the day that your hidden character behaviors will be found out and all you have worked hard for will be forgotten, except for your negative character brightly displayed for all to see. Your company is counting on you to hit those goals, metrics, and strategies, but definitely not at all costs. Your character will be your calling card for years of service with reputable organizations. Take pride in it, and elevate it by your actions. It has been said that people would rather see a sermon than hear one; give your employees, customers, and supervisors something classy to see in you, including how you carry yourself as a leader in regard to character.

When you find yourself in one of the drops, curves, or inclement weather conditions mentioned in the roller-coaster analogy at the onset of this book (and you will in retail), your true character must stand out positively. When those numbers aren't being met and you are faced with opposition from competition, sales, shrink, talent, or staffing, etc., then reflect on this chapter. It will be vital for you to look in the mirror and recognize the leader within and take your team through challenging times in a manner in which they will see your character shine. Remember, retail is ever changing and so will be your daily adversities. Tell the truth in all dealings; your supervisor wants to know and rely on what you say. *The Blind Side* was a great movie, but it is not great for building your servant-leadership character with your employees, customers, supervisors, or company! Make it a personal goal not to blindside people, as a retail leader, with bad news. Be honest as you possibly can in your retail business dealings; it will be the vehicle to take you to your success story!

When you model something, it is on display for all to see; that is the case with your servant-leadership character. Take the time daily to practice listening to the leaders who report to you and the other employees in the building. When they see you as approachable and willing to listen, it will resonate well with them. After all, they have vital insight to share that can ultimately help your performance as a leader in retail. They may share customer insight, innovative ideas, or best practices that you may never have known about without taking the time to listen. Make it fit into your schedule to get out of the office and on the floor to do what I call "checkups from the neck-ups." Yes, this vital checkup takes you five minutes to gain insight as to how your employees are feeling about you, the job, and the company. In just a five-minute interaction, you can usually assess what kind of day your employees are having. The key is if they are having a great day and are in a good mood; then they will probably reciprocate that mood on to customers. If they aren't having a good day, then you and your leaders want to help solve the issue before they face your customers and pass on any negativity. A servant-leader with brilliant character anticipates how to get the most out of those they lead through strong character that builds up.

When I had the privilege to oversee single-unit locations in retail, I inspired all my direct reports to follow the same process or model this behavior. Upon entering the building every day, it was the first thing we did before checking e-mail, merchandise, displays, etc. We made a quick round and talked to every employee, shook hands, and did our five-minute checkup. In one year's time, the store was known as one of the top culture stores in the district and one of the top in the company on employee engagement. It was a simple process; however, the servant-leadership character of taking the time to say hello daily and validate that they were okay and excited to be there led to great results in culture and metrics!

Your company will often change initiatives, strategies, and plans. A servant-leader that is brilliant will not address their team through what I call "third-party management." For example, avoid saying, "The company wants us to do this or change that in the building." A servant-leader will put the message in their own words. The team you lead sees you as the leader, not the company; tailor your message so it is positive and received as a win to get the desired outcome. You can have a respectful discussion about the change with your supervisor, but your team doesn't have to see an attitude from you about it that is less than brilliant. People will most often remember what you do, not what you say! Be an advocate for the company, a change agent. Our world is changing rapidly, and companies will have to change constantly to remain relevant. Be the change you wish to see in others!

Lastly, trust but validate what is important to you as a leader. Your character is on display as a model. As a leader, don't find yourself thinking that some project is done or that some expectation from your supervisor's assignment is complete when you delegated it to someone else. This will impact your character, and you won't even know it is about to happen.

CONCLUDING REMARKS

When you inspect what you expect as a servant-leader, it provides you a great opportunity to commend those who performed well and correct behaviors that are negatively impacting your business. Your retail leadership character will be made up of an essential ingredient called endurance. You will be tested at many levels as a retail leader. Take a breath, and reflect on these eight simple chapters you have read. As authors, we have shared with you some basic insights to help your retail career be successful. We have combined over fifty years of retail experience into this book, what we have seen and witnessed with our own eyes. Most people will pick a career they are passionate about to spend many years of service in. For us, it was retail, and we have loved the ride.

You, dear friend, have chosen well! Strap in, buckle up, and enjoy the ride of your life. We truly wish you all the best in your adventure; enjoy the view from the top as a Brilliant Leader in Retail!

APPENDIX

CHAPTER ONE: BE STAGE READY

Rate the following 1–5 (5 being the best presentation for customers and employees):

1. How clean is your retail parking lot where you work as a leader? _____
2. How clean are your sidewalks from gum, trash, etc., before entering the building? _____

3. Does your merchandising scream excitement and relevance to the demographic shoppers? _____

4. How does the dress and groom of the employees represent the company brand? _____

5. Does every employee who will interact with customers have a smile and a helpful attitude? _____

6. Do the location and every aisle look and smell clean? _____

7. How do the bathrooms look every hour you are open? _____

8. What does the breakroom look like? The microwave? The coffee pot? The fridge? The table? _____

9. What does your office look like? All offices? Organized? Clean? Neat? Inviting? _____

10. What is the culture in the building? Attitude? Team synergy and excitement? _____

11. Do the scheduled employees for the day understand the goals? Expectaions? Standards? _____

12. What does the backroom look like? Organized? Clean? _____

13. What does the area behind your building look like? Trash dumps? Other retailers? _____

14. What does your staffing schedule vs. the business needs look like for the day? _____

15. How does your product in stock or availability look? Ad quantities? _____

Ask the leader to average their score on the questions. Is it 1–2, 3–4, or a 5? If it is not a 4.5 or better, what action plans need to be put in place with urgency to raise the score to "stage ready"? (Utilize the SMART action plan concept discussed in chapter four of this book.)

These fifteen questions will be a great compass to gauge your stage readiness for the day.

CHAPTER TWO: BE AGILE

What special project can you lead or develop to impact on the company strategies?

_____

_____

_____

What are the top three priorities your supervisor is focused on that you could take ownership of and maintain along with your current responsibilities?

_____

_____

_____

How are you promoting innovation and ideas that will keep you ahead of your competition?

_____

_____

_____

What quarterly actionable tasks can you commit yourself to that will differentiate you from your peer group?

_____

_____

_____

CHAPTER THREE: BE KNOWLEDGEABLE

Let's talk knowing your business. The questions below will test your knowledge of your business. Ready, set, answer:

1. What is your store's sales budget this week?

    _____

2. What department/area of the business is exceeding their budget?

    _____

3. What department/area of the business is behind against their budget?

    _____

4. How is your store's business compared to last year? (Year Over Year/YOY)

    _____

5. How did your business unit perform last quarter? (BU)

    _____

6. Do you have a bonus incentive? If so what is it measured on?

    _____

7. How much does it cost to onboard a new employee?

    _____

8. How much "SHRINK" occurred in your store last month?

    _____

9. How often does your P&L store operating statement post?

_____

10. How much does your parent company generate in annual sales?

_____

11. What is your competition doing right?

_____

12. When was your last visit to your competitors?

_____

13. What notes did you take and share that were brilliant to be better than your competitors?

_____

How many did you answer without researching? One? Five? All thirteen?

CHAPTER FOUR: BE COMMUNICATIVE

Role-play giving effective feedback with the following individuals. Think about the **Three Ws** (What's the Situation? What's the Behavior? What's the Impact?):

- A direct report

- A peer

- Your supervisor (boss)

- One level above your boss

Review the last seven days of e-mails you sent or received.

Look for the **Three Is** discussed in the chapter. Break down your e-mails into three categories, using tick marks:

Inform	Inspire	Inflame

If the majority of the e-mails informed, consider yourself an effective communicator.

If the majority of your e-mails inspired, you have demonstrated brilliant characteristics in communication (give yourself a pat on the back).

Reflect on the e-mails you sent that inflamed, and consider these three questions: What steps, if any, do you need to take to reverse course? How will you draft e-mails going forward to ensure they don't inflame but inspire? Out of the e-mails sent that inflamed, what was the result or outcome(s)?

If you received an e-mail that inflamed, what actions will you take today with the sender to provide constructive feedback that could potentially help them communicate more effectively and would result in a better outcome?

CHAPTER FIVE: BE ACCOUNTABLE

Now that you understand the benefits of having an accountability partner, who are the first three to five people that come to your mind that would fit the role? Write down their names.

_____

_____

_____

By what date will you contact them and request that they be your accountability partner (after explaining from the chapter what an effective accountability partner does and why you chose them)?

_____

_____

_____

What will you specifically ask them to hold you accountable for in order to improve in your professional development? Business results?

_____

_____

_____

How will you track and measure improvement?

_____

_____

_____

CHAPTER SIX: BE A NETWORKER

Look at your cell phone and see who are in the top ten calls from the previous week.

Write them down.

_____

_____

_____

How many of your calls would you say were to your peers at work? _____

How many of your calls were to people with the same title or position at your company? _____

How many of your calls were to people with different titles and responsibilities than you have? _____

Write down whom you would call in your network if you were:

- Seeking a promotion
- Having a crisis on the job
- Needing personal advice
- Wanting to change careers

Write down in numerical order people you consider in your network.

_____

_____

_____

After making that list, determine if it is an **open-ended network** (people of all different areas of the business), **closed-ended network** (people with your same title, position, and thought), or **deep-relationship network** (people you can count on for support in a mutually beneficial relationship that will always be there for you).

Write down whom you need in your network to help you achieve your career aspirations.

_____

_____

_____

By what date will you share with your accountability peer that this person or these people will be in your network?

_____

Who is your mentor?

_____

Who is your advisor?

_____

Who is your advocate?

_____

If you don't have one or all three by _____, when will you ask someone to fill that role for you in your leadership career path?

CHAPTER SEVEN: BE JOB READY

Name:
Store:
Position:
Annual Performance Rating:

BE THE SELECTED OR WINNING CANDIDATE

Areas of Development:
1.
2.
3.
4.
5.
6.
7.

Network Wheel:

Stretch Assignments: :

Books to Grow Your Knowledge:

1.

2.

3.

4.

5.

Signature:

CHAPTER EIGHT: BE A SERVANT-LEADER

When will you have round-table listening sessions with your key stakeholders (employees and customers)?

Write down three things you plan to do to lead differently to be a true servant-leader. Share those with your accountability peer. Set check-in dates to measure your progress.

_____

_____

_____

Do a start, stop, and continue exercise with your direct reports to validate your leadership character (each quarter).

_____

_____

_____

_____

_____

_____

_____

Write on a flip chart the following, and leave the room with a designated scribe:

1. What would you like to see me start doing as a leader?
2. What would you like to see me stop doing as a leader?
3. What would you like to see me continue doing as a leader?

Your direct reports will provide you with honest feedback that will help mold you into the servant-leader you want to be and be perceived as (create a culture of safe zone to express their honest opinions of you as their supervisor).

ABOUT THE AUTHOR

I'm happy to say I was born and raised in a very small town in East Texas called Wolfe City. I can tell you I had a rich experience full of love, kindness, and inspiration from my mom, grandparents, family, friends, mentors, teachers, and advisors, from elementary school to East Texas State University.

I can also tell you that that support, inspiration, and guidance allowed me, in my retail career, the privilege of overseeing twenty-seven of the fifty states in America in regards to multiunit retail operational leadership and human-resource retail leadership with various organizations, ranging from small regional businesses to Fortune 500 companies, including the world's largest retailer.

Those are pretty significant achievements. However, the greatest achievement I hope to obtain in my retail career is humbly assisting others to make retail a Brilliant career choice with Brilliant results as a leader! When one person has a better career in retail leadership based off the insight shared in this book, I will feel successful as an author!

Sincerely,

Kelvin Goss

COLOSSIANS 3:23